July 2023

Miah's Monthly Poetry

S. H. Miah

CONTENTS

Newsletter

For writing updates and info on new releases, sign up to our newsletter!

1

SECOND MONTH

The second month, the second collection.

Something about this whole thing feels daunting.

Have I bitten off more than I can chew? Or

Can you bite anything off, as long as your mouth widens?

2

PAIN

Pain on my body

Feels a certain way.

Stabbing, gouging,

But it eventually goes away.

But the pain in my heart,

From loss, from grief, from decay.

That feels much worse,

Like my heart is constrained.

My chest tightens, throat clenches shut.

And it feels like my air ducts

Are blocked, lungs have stopped,

Breathless, the ache in my emotions

Is relentless, and everything I've bottled

Up comes pouring down, an angsty crescendo.

3

LOVE

A mother's love feels never ending.

Never relenting. Always extending.

Despite her anger, her love shines

Brighter than a bursting star.

But Allah's love is greater for us

Than a thousand supernovas

All exploding at once. Do we respect Him

As much as he deserves? Or is our

Gratitude down in the dumps?

4

SNICKERS

I'm chewing a snickers bar.

Nuts and chocolate, all rolled into

One delightful delicacy.

And then I realise that my mouth

Currently holds more ingredients than

Someone's entire fridge.

5
Comparisons

She used to miss him once upon a time.

She used to think he could've been the one.

They were sneaking around East London,

Living it up. Or that's just what she thought.

He used to make advances, say it was time,

But a part of her was protected by Allah.

And she never gave that up. She told him

To ask her dad. But he never did, said they'd

Marry eventually. But she now knows

He only wanted one thing.

And now that she's married, to a faithful husband,

She realised that what she was missing,

Her old boyfriend could never give.

6

For all

I'm studying Arabic now.

Trying to understand the meanings.

It's so elegant yet complex,

Just like our religion.

Those with simple minds

And scholars alike

Can find peace within

The walls of Islam.

A religion for all

That choose to submit

To the way of their Lord.

7

STREAMS

Rain runs through

Streams to reach rivers.

Could we be the stream

For someone else's ocean?

8

FOOTSTEPS

He used to be besotted

With the girl at the end of

The street. They used to

Hang out, loiter about,

Smoking shisha and weed.

They did *haram*,

Things he can't think about.

Then they moved house,

And he stopped seeing her.

And he realised how much

Time he'd wasted,

Following the footsteps

Of Shaytan.

9

ENDS

O Muslim,

Do not be excited

When a non-muslim praises

Islam.

Indeed, if they die upon

Disbelief,

They will be thrown

Into Jahannam.

10
INTERNAL BLEEDING

O Believers,

The ummah is one body.

We may suffer attacks from outside,

But why is our

Internal bleeding

Part of our strife?

11

FAMILY

A family is more than

Just Mum and Dad

And Bro and Sis.

A family is not just

Those you call next of kin.

A family is your blood,

Your genes flow through theirs.

Your family will be yours,

Always closer than those "friends".

12
Chicken wings

Chicken wings,

Chicken wings,

Chicken wings,

Why are you so

Delectable with chips?

Every time I walk past

You, the taste flits to my lips.

I begin to salivate,

My heart rate begins to race,

And my mind chants,

Like it's at a rave.

Chicken wings,

Chicken wings,

Chicken wings.

13

LONE SHEEP

When you find yourself binging,

It's not with other people about.

Hang around with brothers and sisters

Who surround you with goodness.

Because the lone sheep is the

One that the wolf attacks first.

14

Love like Zamzam

When my mother returns from work

I see the exhaustion clawing her skin,

She comes in, eyebags clutching her face.

Closes the door behind her, doesn't climb

The stairs. Instead, walks in the living room,

Hugs us all one by one, and I feel the love

Flowing like the well of *Zamzam*.

15

FA Cup

Watching football.

The FA Cup Final.

Luckily, there's no prayer

In the middle.

I'm asking myself

Whether I would go or not.

What else would I sacrifice

For the sake of entertainment?

16

DEAD WHILST LIVING

A vase sits in the corner,

Purple and pink petals perched

Perfectly inside.

Two sofas, brown and leather,

Weathered by the weights

Of those who sat on them.

A coffee table, with a rug

Atop it, patterns woven within.

A wall with a painting,

Draped onto hooks

Nailed in like a coffin.

A picturesque living room,

But the people inside,

Might as well be in a coffin.

17

UPSIDE DOWN

Losing is the worst feeling.

Working, so hard, only to

Come up short at the end.

But when it comes to Allah,

It's the effort that counts,

The intention that must be sound.

And so every loss can be

Turned upside down.

18

Help

The people we push away

Are the likeliest to return

When life streaks a burn

And we need help at every turn.

19

REALISATIONS

He realises,

When he comes home early one day

And sees her feed her crying babe—

Their crying babe—and quell those wailing tears.

He realises,

When he sees her wake up at night,

Before the sun rises, to pray for

The rewards of their sacrifice.

He realises,

When he watches her haul a sack of potatoes

To the kitchen, slice and dice, before facing fumes

In the face, all so he can eat a warm meal.

He realises,

When he notices her eyes droop, exhaustion

Weighing those lids down, her face in a frown,

But she plasters a smile so as not to seem down.

He realises,

When her eyes light up at the mention of his success.

But with her everyday wins, he says not a word.

He realises how ungrateful he always is.

20

OUTFIT

The value of the outfit

You're wearing at this very second

Likely costs more than someone

Else's entire yearly income.

21

Charity

Sadaqah jaariyah

Is the best investment.

It pays enormous dividends

In both of our existences.

22

Provisions

When I look back at my life,

So much of Allah's provisions for me

Came from sources least expected.

I guess we can't truly be grateful for our blessings

Until our minds flick back in reflection, and our introspection

Reveals the same.

23

BRITISH

A cup of tea

Steams before me.

The foam releases

Smoke that is elevating.

Though my parents are

Immigrants, tea and a biscuit,

Still makes me feel British.

It is, sadly, perhaps, the only thing.

24

DAWAH

We have the guidance

On how to reach Paradise.

Why do we not have the urge

To spread this guidance to humanity?

Is it that we don't have the zeal

To save them along with ourselves?

Is it that our only dawah is through character?

An excuse we use without knowing what that means.

Learn your religion,

A message to you and I,

And don't be afraid to speak,

For indeed the truth never lies.

25

Gather round

Gather round,

Gather round,

There's a Muslim abound.

And guess what? He's actually

Done something of which to be proud.

Guess what it is. I bet

It'll never be found.

He's a footballer, a boxer,

Famous in the Instagram crowds.

Yeah, I know he's not a scholar,

But at least he can rainbow flick.

And I know he's not a hafiz,

But he can fight karate with sticks.

I know he's not helping Allah,

And uses *haram* music,

But at least he's a Muslim right,

Having some kind of influence?

Gather round for the spectacle.

Finally, a Muslim we can use

For the 'better'. We don't care if he's actually religious,

As long as he somewhat fits our agenda.

26

CARDS

We've all been dealt our cards in life.

And in fact, our future cards have already been dealt.

We can't throw them away for new kings and jacks.

But in Jannah, we will have an unlimited amount of decks.

So don't use *haram* means, in this world, for new packs.

27

FRESH FOREVER

At *iftar* that first sip of crisp water

Feels like heaven in a glass,

Like a ray of sunshine piercing

An arctic hibernation.

Imagine, then, that in Jannah

Everything will feel fresher, for eternity,

Than even that fresh, first sip.

28 It was always you

I thought I would never stop hating you.

But once I learned your childhood, learned the context

Within which your toxicity was born, I understood.

I don't forgive you, at least not now, but at least

I can find peace within my heart, knowing

It was never me—*never* me—and it was always you.

29
DROWNING

The abuse he feels

Feels like my own.

I want to help, but

Every story he tells

Sinks him deeper

Into a spiral of depression.

We are both in an ocean

Of his anxiety.

He is swimming, whilst

I am the boat pushing

Against the tide.

But perhaps the pull of

The ocean is too strong,

And it will drown

Both of us inside.

30
GREATER TREASURES

She remembers when she first met him.

Her father was beside her, monitoring

The meeting. But that didn't stop

The light smile from freckling his cheeks,

The squinting eyes behind those glasses,

Mesmerisingly green. The hard set shoulders

And soft, wavy hair. But when they

Actually got married, she found the appearances

Were only an invitation to far greater treasures

Within his heart.

31

Bearings

Sometimes, I wonder

How you could bear me

For nine, long months,

When I can barely bear myself

Any more after lunch.

32

PACKED LUNCHES

I remember the packed lunches you packed

With packets of capri sun and

A packet of crisps. Packed in those packages

Was a labour of love, every lunch without fail.

33

BAILIFF

Stabs of guilt pierce me,

When I look at your face once more.

Some deeds cannot be undone,

So all I have left is to raise my hands,

In supplication to Allah.

I pray that He gives you Jannah, pray

That the best thereafter graces your

Hereafter. Perhaps, my fervent dua

Will convince you not to become the bailiff,

Knocking at my crumbling sandcastle of deeds.

34

Bygones

There was once a time

When your presence felt like

The highlight of my life.

Now, perhaps it is I

Who feels dead inside.

Or maybe you were the one who died.

Either way, what's left has gone by,

Bygones of the past.

35

GENUINE

Have you seen the way

A baby giggles?

Its eyes lighting up,

Smile so wide all its

Teeth are visible.

Perhaps, for many of us,

That was the last time

We showed any genuine happiness.

36

DUVET

A duvet protects us when we sleep,

From the harshness of the night,

The wailing winds and coldness seeping in,

Whilst we slumber in dreamy delight.

Our religion is like a duvet, a garment shielding us,

From the roughness and harshness of the world.

Everyone else is lost, whilst we have the guidance

From our Lord. It is a gift, so be grateful most of all.

37
STANDING

How many of us

Give standing ovations,

Or stand out of respect

For an elder or minister,

But don't stand for Allah

Whether in the day or night,

In either good or bad times,

Even when the loss we suffer

Is a limitless paradise?

38

WATER

Have you ever contemplated

The blessing of water?

To those who believe there is no Allah:

How is it that a liquid has popped

Into existence, perfectly for us?

Life is built on water—fine.

But what is water built on?

You must realise that, in the end,

Everything stems back to the Lord.

39

ATONEMENT

You looked her in the eyes. The friend you betrayed.

You see the hurt, the pain, and regret what you can never wash away.

But you stay, supporting that friend, despite your past sins.

Because atonement is something we must all yearn for, in the end.

40
Creations

Man made creations

Need symmetry for beauty.

When was the last time

You saw a perfectly symmetrical tree?

41

Vehicles

Hope can be a driving force

Towards good. But it is not

The only vehicle we can take.

Why do you think Allah speaks

Of heaven and hell?

Because our fear of hell

Can drive us towards Him

Just the same.

42 CANNOT HAVE

We yearn for what we cannot have.

Hence, sometimes when my eyes fall

On a brand new Tesla, or a supercharged Ford,

Or the latest phone or superstar Nike Jords,

I glance away. Staring in absolute awe

Will only light the fire of ungratefulness in my core.

43

Don't sleep

It's late at night.

I know I should sleep.

But something's keeping me awake.

I turn over in bed,

Shift my duvet,

Then reach a hand over to grab

The source of all pain.

I turn it on,

Screen blares into my eyes.

I go on YouTube like

It's a digital paradise.

I have to wake for *fajr* soon,

And I've got work in the morning.

But I start the nightly binge.

Autoplay is my friend.

In the end,

I don't wake up in time.

I've traded this life

For the havens of heaven.

44
TAKING TURNS

Some people

Are only backstabbers

When you turn your

Back on them.

45
Reciprocation

Some people you love

And the love is not reciprocated.

Your heart aches, with the pain

Of what could've been, what you lost.

And the subsequent suffering is the cost.

But Allah—his love is greater than

Anything we can imagine.

When we truly love Him

And love for His sake,

We find in all our love

Reciprocation.

46

Returns

Those minutes and seconds that

Tick by,

With every moment,

Even as you read this,

Will never return.

With every breath

You take,

Realise the thing

Getting closer

Is not time's return,

But yours.

47
OFTEN

Why do we so often

Stare back at our life

And wish to fill it with nostalgia?

Why do we so often

Glare at our present

And wish it was like the past?

Why do we so often

Rue our future as if

We have no hope in Allah?

48

Hurricane

Sometimes I write

Like the wind in a hurricane.

The wind, perhaps, knows

Its moment of tumultuous

Glory will soon be over.

So it must attempt

To have the most effect

With the little time

It has left.

49

LOST

I often think of

Something to say.

And then never write it down,

Never let the words leave my mind.

And it could be one of the best

Quotes in all of mankind.

But it flits past my attention,

And no amount of yearning

In the world could ever

Retrieve those lost thoughts.

50

Thin line

I know I am loved

By my friends and family.

But perhaps, one of my biggest fears

Is leaving this *dunya* whilst

They have a grudge against me.

Because there is a thin line

Between love and hate.

We could be standing on opposite

Sides on that fateful day,

And they will ask me to pay

With my good deeds,

Which will drift away.

51

IMPROVE

First we couldn't move,

Then we crawled,

Then we stumbled,

Then we walked,

Then we ran.

Why have some of us

Not improved beyond that?

52
EMOTIONS

Emotions aren't just mere chemicals in the body.

You feel it, don't you?

The warmth in your chest when you see someone you love?

The pounding of your heart when push turns to shove?

The sinking of your stomach when you find out your friend

Has betrayed you and now you feel that feeling dig in?

The laughter and joy you feel when with your best friend?

The love that extends when you ruffle your child's head?

Emotions also exist in Jannah.

So do not assume that they are mere chemicals.

Indeed, your love for your mother

Is a feeling that can cross between worlds.

53

SPONTANEITY

We can plan and plan,

From Eid to Eid to Eid once again,

The changes we wish to take place.

But it is our laziness that causes

A spontaneous shift in our life.

Sometimes, tragedy can be a blessing

In disguise. A device to alter you

Into a better self, so you

May enter Paradise.

54
Expressions

I'm in bed, shrouded by dark

As I write this. It's odd—

The fact that dark can be

Just as expressive as lightness.

55

Meaning

My spine tingles

And the hairs on my arm

Stand on end

When the Qur'an is being recited.

My soul would probably

Fly from my body

And enter another realm,

If I truly grasped the meaning.

56
RECITATION

It's odd,

Yet makes complete sense,

That my most productive days,

When writing or studying,

Always begin

With Qur'an recitation.

Yet for some strange reason,

I don't hasten towards it.

57
SLEEP

Every night,

When you sleep,

Your soul leaves your body.

And the only reason you wake up

Is because Allah allowed your soul's return.

Every night then, in reality,

Is merely a miniature death,

Leading to our ultimate demise.

58
OPPORTUNITY

We live in realms of opportunity.

Our issue is we don't see the chances

Allah gives us to change our behaviour

To turn back to him with repentance.

Instead we languish in our heedlessness.

I've wronged someone, and yet every time I see them

I skirt past the apology I know they deserve

And I know I should give. An opportunity missed.

When I see the sadness in your eyes

And I know it's what I've caused, why does my ego

Block those words from exiting my throat

Even though my heart can say them out loud?

Even when alone, I feel like I'm in a crowd

Of thoughts, circling my head. Sometimes

I write them down, get them out into the world.

Yet those opportunities remain, lonely and untaken.

How many more will Allah give me?

How many more will I ignore?

59

Circles

Many times in my life

I experience movement.

Improvement, perhaps.

But in the end,

When I look back,

I realise I've just been moving,

In circles.

60

ARABIC

I'm studying Arabic now.

And the language is so beautiful

Its beauty eclipses everything

Else in my life. The words

Carry so much more depth

Than I first realised.

And now, though my understanding

Still borders on beginner,

The Qur'an's recitation

Carries a whole other

Realm of meaning.

61

Tesco meal deal

I remember when Tesco first created their meal deals.

I grabbed the cheese and tomato pasta, the Sensations crisps, and the Oasis

Since Mum never let me have any kind of fizzy drinks.

I took it home, popped open the pasta, and realised with delight

That it had a little fork hidden inside. I pierced the plastic film

Covering the top, then ripped it fully open, then pushed in the fork.

The pasta was amazing, delicate on the tongue. It was only three pounds

But felt like it deserved to be a hundred.

Sensations was my favourite crisps, crispy with spice.

I wolfed down the entire packet, almost in one bite.

Then came the Oasis, like an oasis of flavours

Exploding out loud. And even now,

Years and years later, I'm sitting at my laptop,

Writing this collection, with a Tesco meal deal in my mouth.

62
LOFTINESS

I remember receiving the advice,

So long ago, that in my life

I should set lofty goals.

I read the biographies of the past scholars

And sometimes my mind explodes

At how productive they were,

At how much they achieved in such

Short spans of time. Then, I realise

That in the grand scheme of things,

My poetry collection every month really is,

In a large ocean, a small fish.

63

COMPARE

The scholars of the past

Died when being persecuted

For their religion.

And yet we fear what people

Will say, so we stay seated

Amongst the few that stand up.

64

GIFT

Our religion is the greatest

Gift we could've been given.

Everyone is in an identity drift,

Not knowing who or what they are.

Confusion is rife, everyone believes they're right.

But Allah, in the end, is The Truth.

And it is His Power and Might

That reigns over us all.

So, the next time you and I

Find ourselves facing a wall

Of islamophobia from those

Who don't understand Islam at all,

Remember the gift you've been given,

Because it is more precious

Than a diamond or even the crown jewels.

65

WHAT JUST HAPPENED?

There's a feeling

That is very hard to describe.

When you wake up in

The morning with the foggiest mind.

And then you wake up again,

And when you check the time,

It's gone back an hour, and you

Wonder what on earth has just happened?

66

Imagine

Feelings are what make life

Feel worth living.

Can you imagine your mother,

Without the love between you and her?

Can you imagine your Muslim brother

Without loving him for the sake of Allah?

Can you imagine the bleakness of a world

In which there is only pitiless indifference?

67

Nonsense

Some people attempt to suggest

That there is no Allah, is no Creator,

And that morality is just pitiless indifference.

Just think about it for a second—the stars,

The earth, all the beauty we see,

Came from blind, unexplained processes?

What a load of nonsense!

68
ISLAM

Islam

Is not a cloak we wear.

Islam

Is not merely words on the tongue.

Islam

Is not praying here and there.

Islam

Is not taking this life as merely fun.

Islam

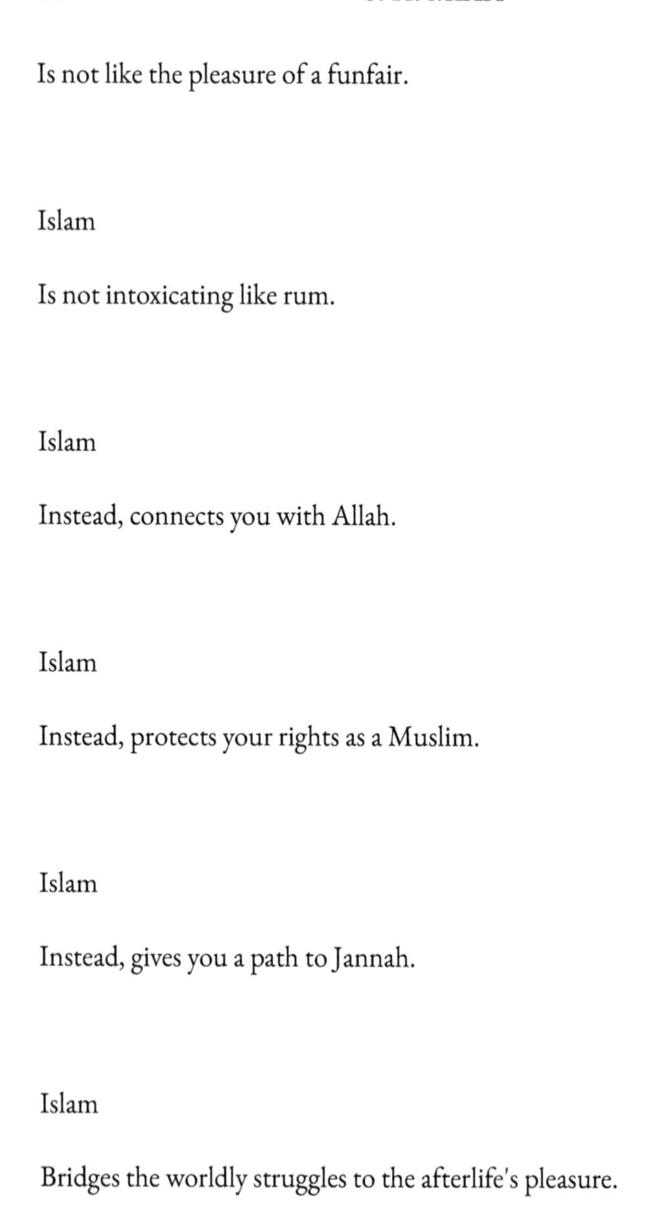

Is not like the pleasure of a funfair.

Islam

Is not intoxicating like rum.

Islam

Instead, connects you with Allah.

Islam

Instead, protects your rights as a Muslim.

Islam

Instead, gives you a path to Jannah.

Islam

Bridges the worldly struggles to the afterlife's pleasure.

Islam

Is our way of life, mighty and strong.

Islam

Is nothing embarrassing, so be proud of your religion.

Islam

In the end, is the ultimate salvation.

69

ROUTES

We memorise the routes

To certain places in our mind.

Like work or school,

We know exactly where they are.

We can trace the path

In our heads, up the road

And around the bend.

And it's only because

We've interacted with

This route so many times.

Why is it, then, that

We get lost on our

Path back to repentance?

Is it because it's a route

We seldom ever take?

70

Take

Take, take, take,

Take some more.

My time is a lake,

Dip your buckets in and

Take as much as you want.

Don't worry about how tired

I get, don't worry about my feelings.

Just keep taking more, and even more,

And let me continue sinking.

71

TIME WASTE

I used to play video games

From five to six to ten hours a day.

Now I regret all the time that I wasted.

Imagine if I wrote now as I did then.

I probably would have come out

With ten thousand poetry collections.

72

Dark times

Sometimes love feels like an aeroplane

Flying high above the world.

Other times, dark times,

I'm swimming in the ocean,

Not knowing where to go,

Or even if there exists a shore.

73

MIRACLE

When you feel alone,

When you feel like

There's no one for you.

Just pray to Allah,

And believe that the

Creator of the worlds

Can bring the perfect

Person to you, even if

From across the globe.

74

Sincere

Have you ever raised your hands

To Allah, and made a sincere *dua*?

Was it not accepted?

Indeed, the issue lies

With us, not Allah.

If we were truly sincere,

Our blessings would

Rise, in our eyes,

From the earth

To the stars.

75

Heart to heart

Poetry collections

Are sweet and short.

As writers, we try to encapsulate

Feelings, insulate them

And watch them grow,

Then express them in either

Elegant prose, or crafted verse.

And transfer what is in our hearts,

To yours.

Newsletter

For writing updates and info on new releases, sign up to our newsletter!

ABOUT MFP

The Muslim Fiction Project, MFP, is an initiative started by S. H. Miah to publish works of fiction that promote Islamic messages for Muslims all around the world.

Written for Muslims. By a Muslim.

Visit our website to see what other stories you could sink your teeth into!

About S. H. Miah

S. H. Miah is the founder of Muslim Fiction Project. An initiative to produce high-quality Muslim fiction. Written for Muslims. By a Muslim.

When not writing, S. H. Miah enjoys spending time with family and friends, charging through his own reading list, and of course having a bit too large an obsession with spiral-bound notebooks.

For more information about Muslim Fiction Project, please visit: https://www.muslimfictionproject.com

Ingram Content Group UK Ltd.
Milton Keynes UK
UKHW020631200723
425492UK00016B/594